The Scripture Practice

A Four-Session Guide to Reading the Bible as an Apprentice to Jesus

WaterBrook

John Mark Comer and Practicing the Way

A WaterBrook Trade Paperback Original

Published in the United States by WaterBrook, an imprint of the Penguin Random House Christian Publishing Group, a division of Penguin Random House LLC, 1745 Broadway, New York, NY 10019.

WaterBrook and colophon are registered trademarks of Penguin Random House LLC.

Published in association with Yates & Yates, www.yates2.com.

All photos courtesy of Practicing the Way.

Trade Paperback ISBN 978-0-593-60335-2
Ebook ISBN 978-0-593-60336-9

Printed in the United States of America on acid-free paper

waterbrookmultnomah.com
penguinrandomhouse.com

1st Printing

Book and cover design by Practicing the Way

For details on special quantity discounts for bulk purchases, contact specialmarketscms@penguinrandomhouse.com.

The authorized representative in the EU for product safety and compliance is Penguin Random House Ireland, Morrison Chambers, 32 Nassau Street, Dublin D02 YH68, Ireland, https://eu-contact.penguin.ie.

Contents

PART 01

Getting Started

Welcome

Were not our hearts burning within us while he talked with us on the road and opened the Scriptures to us?

—Luke 24v32

At the center of human history is a person—Jesus the Christ, the Son of God. Until very recently, much of the world measured time itself by the years leading up to and following his birth. And since the earliest days of the community of Jesus, the library of writings called the Bible have been central to the lives of Jesus' followers.

Written over more than a thousand years, by dozens of different authors, and in multiple languages and genres of literature, the Bible can sometimes feel like a bewildering maze of history and poetry and laws and letters and more.

Yet when you put it all together, you realize this collection of writings tells one long, cohesive story that leads us to Jesus.

But we don't read this library the way we read the daily news or a social media caption or even other books. In fact, the digital age has rewired our brains, making it very difficult for us to read Scripture the way it was *designed* to be read—slowly, deeply, prayerfully. At times, communally.

We created this Practice to help you learn how to read Scripture as a spiritual discipline, as a way of meeting God on every page and opening your spirit to his Spirit to heal and change you from the inside out.

This will require us to learn to read Scripture *as apprentices of Jesus*, not just for *information*, but also for *formation*. It will require us to rewire our brains so they can deeply attune to God's speaking voice as we read. And it will require us to make immersing our minds and hearts in Scripture a practice, a daily discipline of love.

The Nine Practices

SABBATH

PRAYER

FASTING

SOLITUDE

GENEROSITY

SCRIPTURE

COMMUNITY

SERVICE

WITNESS

The Scripture Practice is just one of nine core Practices in the body of resources available from Practicing the Way. The Practices are spiritual disciplines centered around the life rhythms of Jesus. They are designed not to add even more to your already overbusy life, but to slow you down and create space for the Spirit of God to form you to be with Jesus, become like him, and do what he did. Ultimately, they are a way to experience the love of God.

To run another Practice or learn more, turn to page 108.

How to Use This Guide

A few things you need to know

This Practice is designed to be done in community, whether with a few friends around a table, within your small group, in a larger class format, or with your entire church.

The Practice is four sessions long. We recommend meeting together every week or every other week. For those of you who want to spend more time on this Practice, we've included an additional four weeks of bonus conversations in the appendix to go deeper in Scripture and discussion. You are welcome to pause for these conversations in between sessions or skip over them.

You will all need a copy of this Companion Guide. You can purchase a print or ebook version from your preferred book retailer. We recommend the print version so you can stay away from your devices during the Practices, as well as take notes during each session. But we realize that digital works better for some.

Each session should take about one to two hours, depending on how long you set aside for discussion and whether or not you begin with a meal. See the sample session on the following page.

Are you a group leader or facilitator? See page 112 for helpful information and additional ideas and tips on running this Practice.

Our Practices are designed to work in a variety of group sizes and environments. For that reason, your gatherings may include additional elements like meals or worship time, or may follow a structure slightly different from the following sample. Please adapt as you see fit.

Sample Session

Here is what a typical session could look like.

Welcome

Welcome the group and open in prayer.

Introduction (2–3 min.)

Watch the introduction and pause the video when indicated for your first discussion.

Discussion 01: Practice reflection in triads (15–20 min.)

Process your previous week's spiritual exercise in smaller groups of three to five people with the questions in the Guide.

Teaching (20 min.)

Watch the teaching portion of the video.

Discussion 02: Group conversation (15–30 min.)

Pause the video when indicated for a group-wide conversation.

Testimony and tutorial (5–10 min.)

Watch the rest of the video.

Prayer to close

Close by praying the liturgy in the Guide, or however you choose.

The Weekly Rhythm

The four sessions of this Practice are designed to follow a four-part rhythm that is based on our model of spiritual formation.

Learn
about the Way of Jesus.

IN COMMUNITY

Process together
what is coming up for you through your experience.

WEEKLY RHYTHM

Practice
with spiritual exercises using your Companion Guide.

ON YOUR OWN

Reflect
on your experience with God.

01 Learn

Gather together as a community for an interactive experience of learning about the Way of Jesus through teaching, storytelling, and discussion. Bring your Guide to the session and follow along.

02 Practice

On your own, before the next session, go and "put it into practice," as Jesus himself said.* We will provide weekly spiritual exercises to integrate this Practice into your everyday life, as well as recommended resources to go deeper.

03 Reflect

Reflection is key to spiritual formation. After your practice and before the next session, set aside 10–15 minutes to reflect on your experience. Reflection questions are included in this Guide at the end of each session.

04 Process together

When you come back together, watch the introduction, and then start by sharing your reflections with your group. This moment is crucial because we need each other to process our lives before God and make sense of our stories. If you are meeting in a larger group, you will need to break into smaller subgroups for this conversation so everyone has a chance to share.

---

* Philippians 4v9.

Tips on Beginning a New Practice

This Guide is full of spiritual exercises, time-tested strategies, and good advice on reading Scripture as a spiritual practice.

But it's important to note that the Practices are not formulaic. We can't use them to control our spiritual formation or even our relationship with God. Sometimes they don't even work very well. Over the coming weeks, there may be some days when you feel God's voice leap off the page and into your heart, and others when you just feel bored, distracted, and confused. That's normal.

The key with all the spiritual disciplines is to let go of outcomes and just offer them up to Jesus in love.

Because it's so easy to lose sight of the ultimate aim of a Practice, here are a few tips to keep in mind as you engage with Scripture.

01 Start small

Start where you are, not where you "should" be. It's counterintuitive, but the smaller the start, the better chance you have of really sticking to it and growing over time. It's better to read one or two verses every single day, slowly and in a meditative mode, than to try to read through the Bible in three months and crash and burn on day five.

02 Think subtraction, not addition

Don't try to add Scripture into your already overbusy life. You are likely already overwhelmed. Instead, think, *How can I simplify my daily routine to make space for what matters most—being with God and listening for his voice?* Formation is about less, not more. About slowing down and simplifying your life around what's most important: life with Jesus.

03 You get out what you put in

The more fully you give yourself to this Practice, the more life-changing it will be; the more you just dabble in it, the more shortcuts you take, the less of an effect it will have on your transformation. It's up to you: We make invitations; you make decisions.

04 Remember the J curve

Experts on learning tell us that whenever we set out to master a new skill, it tends to follow a J-shaped curve; we tend to get worse before we get better. Reading Scripture can be difficult and intimidating. Like all great literature, at times it's not easy to understand. And when it is, it's even harder to live out. That's okay. Expect it to be a bit difficult at first; it will get easier in time. Just stay with the Practice.

05 There is no formation without repetition

Spiritual formation is slow, deep, cumulative work that happens over years, not weeks. The goal of this four-week experience is just to get you started on a journey of a lifetime. Upon completion of this Practice, you will have a map for the journey ahead and hopefully some possible companions for the Way.

But what you do next is up to you.

Before You Begin

The following resources are designed to broaden your experience of the Scripture Practice, but they are entirely optional.

Recommended reading

Reading a book alongside the Scripture Practice can greatly enhance your understanding and enjoyment of this discipline. You may love to read, or you may not. For that reason, it's recommended but certainly not required.

The recommended reading for the Scripture Practice is *Eat This Book: A Conversation in the Art of Spiritual Reading* by Eugene Peterson.

Eugene H. Peterson (1932–2018) was a pastor, scholar, author, and poet. He wrote more than 30 books, including his widely acclaimed paraphrase of the Bible, *The Message;* his memoir, *The Pastor;* and numerous works of biblical spiritual formation, including *Run with the Horses* and *Traveling Light.*

The Lectio Bible

The Lectio Bible was designed for a distraction-free reading experience: Chapters, verses, and subheadings have been removed, and footnotes are placed at the end of each book so that you can immerse yourself in Scripture with a heart attuned to Jesus.

We specifically created this unique, new edition of Scripture to go along with this Practice.

Learn more and access free reading plans at practicingtheway.org/lectio.

The Spiritual Health Reflection

One final note: Before you begin Session 01, please set aside 20–30 minutes and take the Spiritual Health Reflection. This is a self-assessment we developed in partnership with pastors and leading experts in spiritual formation. It's designed to help you reflect on the health of your soul in order to better name Jesus' invitations to you as you follow the Way.

You can come back to the Spiritual Health Reflection as often as you'd like (we recommend one to two times a year) to chart your growth and continue to move forward on your spiritual journey.

To access the Spiritual Health Reflection, visit practicingtheway.org/reflection and create an account. Answer the prompt questions slowly and prayerfully.

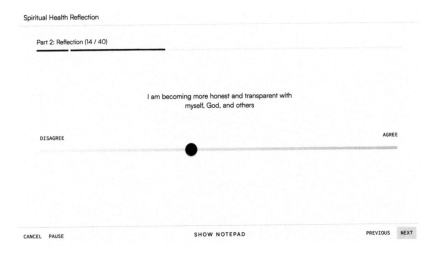

The Practicing the Way primer

If this is your first time engaging with a Practicing the Way resource, we invite you to set aside 15 minutes before Session 01 to watch a primer on spiritual formation. This will give you a brief overview of the *why* behind spiritual practices and key insights to guard and guide your coming practice.

Log in to your online Dashboard or sign up to watch the primer at launch.practicingtheway.org.

PART 02

The Sessions

Read

Overview

Jesus was a rabbi, or a teacher, of the Torah—the Bible of his day. His mind and imagination were saturated in Scripture. Listen to his teachings! They are *full* of quotes, allusions, metaphors, and hyperlinks back to the Hebrew Bible.

Our goal is to read Scripture *as apprentices of Jesus*. This means we don't read it the way we read an online article or textbook chapter or even a literary novel. Unlike other works of literature, *the author is with us in the room*.

Our goal isn't just to *read* Scripture, but also to meet Jesus on the page. To be *with* him, to become *like* him, and to be formed into the people who live out what we read. Or as Jesus put it, "to obey everything I have commanded you."*

That's why our posture is even more important than our technique. We must come to Scripture with the hearts of disciples—sitting at Jesus' feet and listening for his word.

---

* Matthew 28v20.

Opening Questions

When instructed, circle up in triads (smaller groups of three to five people) and discuss the following questions:

01 What brought you to this practice? What are you hoping to see God do in your life through it?

02 Growing up, how did your family regard the Bible?

03 What is your primary feeling about Scripture? Fear? Desire for more? Shame? Ambivalence?

04 How do you see Scripture as a part of your apprenticeship to Jesus?

Teaching

Key Scripture

Do not think that I have come to abolish the Law or the Prophets; I have not come to abolish them but to fulfill them. For truly I tell you, until heaven and earth disappear, not the smallest letter, not the least stroke of a pen, will by any means disappear from the Law until everything is accomplished. Therefore anyone who sets aside one of the least of these commands and teaches others accordingly will be called least in the kingdom of heaven, but whoever practices and teaches these commands will be called great in the kingdom of heaven.

—Matthew 5v17–19

Session summary

- Jesus was clear: His mission was not to abolish the Law or the Prophets but to fulfill them. He embodied and realized the promises of the Old Testament in every way.

- There is a reciprocal relationship between the role of Scripture in our lives and the depth of our formation as Kingdom people. A key part of our apprenticeship to Jesus is allowing Scripture to constantly shape our imaginations, emotions, words, and actions.

- As apprentices, our goal is to be with Jesus, become like him, and do as he did—and each aspect of this goal requires us to regularly immerse our minds and hearts in Scripture.

- Reading Scripture as apprentices of Jesus requires us to read *formationally*, not just *informationally*.

- As we read, it's important to remember that Jesus himself is in the room with us. Our goal is to meet him on every page.

Teaching Notes

As you watch Session 01 together, feel free to use these pages to take notes.

Discussion Questions

Now it's time for a conversation about the teaching. Pause the video for a few minutes to discuss in small groups:

01 What was one insight from the teaching you want to carry with you this coming week?

02 Do you resonate more with reading Scripture for information or formation? Why?

03 Would you consider yourself more of a left-brained person (analytical, rational) or right-brained person (intuitive, symbolic)? How has that impacted the way you read Scripture?

04 What's the primary obstacle you face to the regular reading of Scripture (e.g., time, your sleep habits, parenting, work schedule, intellectual questions, emotional triggers)?

Practice Notes

As you continue to watch Session 01 together, feel free to use this page to take notes.

Closing Prayer

Take a few deep breaths, become aware of God's presence, and pray this prayer slowly, leaving a short silence between each line.

Jesus,

May we receive you personally through your holy Scriptures.

May we read not only with our minds, but also with our hearts.

May we seek relationship more than information.

May we allow ourselves to be wholly shaped by every word.

May we discover the joy and beauty of meeting you here.

Amen.

Exercise

The daily reading of Scripture

- **Find a good *place* that is quiet and distraction-free.** Ideally, choose a spot that makes you happy to be in and that is free of things that might pull at your attention.

- **Find a good *time*.** Choose an unhurried time that feels right for you, allowing space for intentional connection with God.

- **Make a plan for what to read.** Will you explore a gripping narrative from the Old Testament, such as Exodus, Esther, or Jonah? Perhaps you'll reflect on a chapter from the Psalms or Proverbs each day this week. Or maybe you'll begin with one of the New Testament Gospels or one of Paul's letters. See the four recommendations on pages 34–35.

- **Begin by settling your body in God's presence.** Focus your attention on the Father and the Son and the Holy Spirit within you. As Jesus said, "I in them and you in me."*

- **Open in prayer:** "As I open the Scriptures now, I pause to be still, to breathe slowly, to reset my scattered senses upon the presence of God." Remember, the author is in the room with you.

- **Read:** Take in the words slowly. Notice phrases that catch your attention or connect emotionally. God may be highlighting these for your life or the day ahead.

---

* John 17v23.

While the practice of reading Scripture will look unique from person to person, here are a few helpful notes to keep in mind as you shape your practice for the week ahead.

- Consider reaching for a hard copy of the Bible so you can leave your phone in another room to minimize distractions.

- As you read, be mindful not to judge your experience. You may find it deeply meaningful, or perhaps it won't resonate at all. You might feel close to God, or you might not. Simply offer your practice to God in love, allowing it to unfold as it will.

Reach Exercise

We recognize that we're all at different stages of discipleship and seasons of life. To that end, we've added a Reach Exercise to each of the four sessions for those who have the time, energy, and desire to go further in the Scripture Practice.

Read an entire biblical book in one sitting, whether alone or with others from your community.

- Consider selecting a letter from the New Testament—Ephesians, Philippians, or James are great options—but feel free to choose whatever resonates with you.

- If you prefer to experience this in community—following the tradition of God's people throughout church history—gather a few friends in a quiet space. Enjoy a meal or a cup of coffee, then settle into a comfortable spot, invite the Holy Spirit, and read aloud together.

- Afterward, take time to share what stood out to you and pray together.

Four ways of reading Scripture from the best of church history

There are all sorts of different ways to read Scripture; here are four of the most beloved from the global, historic Church:

01 *Lectio Divina*

This is a slow, prayerful, intuitive way of reading Scripture that has long been the hallmark of monastic communities.

We'll devote Session 02 to learning more about this way of reading Scripture that the biblical writers call "meditation."

02 The lectionary

This is the most common approach to the daily reading of Scripture in the Catholic and Anglican traditions, as well as many Protestant streams, like those from the Presbyterian and Lutheran traditions. In this model, you read a daily curation of short verses or passages from the Psalms, the Gospels, the New Testament writings, and key parts of the Old Testament. Over the course of the year, the lectionary is designed to expose you to the major themes of Scripture and to immerse your mind and imagination in the broad sweep of the story of God. If you're interested in following a lectionary, we recommend you explore the Common Lectionary (link.practicingtheway.org/scripture-1a) from Bible Gateway or BREAD (link.practicingtheway.org/scripture-1b) from King's Cross Church in London. For pastors and church leaders, we recommend *A Guide to Prayer for Ministers and Other Servants* by Norman Shawchuck and Rueben P. Job.

03 Reading through the Bible

This approach comes from the evangelical stream of the church. In it, you read a chapter (or a few chapters) every day in a regular quiet time, making your way through the entire Bible from cover to cover. Most versions recommend you do this over a year, but you can amend the timeline to two years or two months, depending on your capacity. This can be a very helpful model for new Christians who are still learning the broad sweep of the Bible. If you choose this option, we recommend you use the reading plan at practicingtheway.org/scripture-1c and follow along with the videos from BibleProject.

04   Hearing Scripture read out loud in community

Finally, there is an approach that is very uncommon today but was the default mode in the early church: hearing longer portions of Scripture read out loud to your community in one sitting.

Take Paul's letter to the church in Ephesus. If you were one of the first followers of Jesus, you would not have pulled out your Bible and read a chapter of Ephesians each day for a week; that was not possible until the invention of the printing press over a thousand years later. You would have gone to your house church on a Sunday night, and after the meal, you would have sat around the home's courtyard, and one of the elders would have read the whole letter to your community. You would likely then talk about it, ask questions of the elders, and pray together. And while we are no longer an oral culture, this way of engaging with Scripture can be deeply formational for both you and your community. You can also augment this approach and read longer portions or entire books of the Bible in one sitting by yourself.

None of these four ways of reading Scripture is the "right" way; you might choose one based on your church tradition, experiment with all four, or make up your own method.

We recommend you follow your joy.

Practice Reflection

Reflection is a key component in our spiritual formation.

Millennia ago, King David prayed in Psalm 139v23–24:

> Search me, God, and know my heart;
> test me and know my anxious thoughts.
> See if there is any offensive way in me,
> and lead me in the way everlasting.

South African professor Trevor Hudson has quoted one of his pastoral supervisors as saying, "We do not learn from experience; we learn from reflection upon experience."*

If you want to get the most out of this Practice, you need to do it and then reflect on it.

———————————

* Trevor Hudson, *A Mile in My Shoes: Cultivating Compassion* (Nashville, Tenn.: Upper Room Books, 2005), 57.

Before your next time together with the group for Session 02, take 10–15 minutes to journal your answers to the following three questions:

01 Where did I feel resistance?

02 Where did I feel joy?

03 Where did I most experience God's nearness?

Note: As you write, be as specific as possible. While bullet points are fine, if you write your insights out in narrative form, your brain will be able to process them in a more lasting way.

Reflection Notes

Keep Growing (Optional)

The following resources were curated to enhance your experience of this Practice, but they are entirely optional.

📖 Read

Eat This Book by Eugene Peterson (Chapters 01–02)

▷ Watch

BibleProject has crafted an incredible series titled How to Read the Bible. This week, we invite you to explore the first part, "Intro to the Bible" (link.practicingtheway.org/scripture-1d), which includes four short episodes:

- What Is the Bible?
- The Story of the Bible
- Literary Styles
- Ancient Jewish Meditation Literature

*Please note: These episodes are only a few minutes long, fun to watch, and very helpful in learning to read Scripture.

ılılı Listen

Rule of Life podcast on Scripture (Episode 01)
Join John Mark as he interviews the BibleProject scholar team.

🖃 Bonus Conversation

If you would like to slow down this four-week Practice to give your community more time to sit in each week's teaching and spiritual exercise, you can pause and meet for an optional conversation outlined in the appendix.

Meditate

Overview

The digital age has rewired our brains and conditioned us to a new style of reading; we're used to quickly skimming over words to get the information we need and then moving on. But this fast, clickbait mode of reading is at odds with the way Scripture was *designed* to be read.

The word used in Scripture for the ideal way the Bible was intended to be read is "meditation," translated from the Hebrew *hagah*. This rich word calls us to a mode of reading that is slow, reflective, and prayerful. German pastor and martyr Dietrich Bonhoeffer defined *meditation* as the "prayerful consideration of Scripture."*

While there is no single way to meditate on Scripture, there is a practice that over the centuries has risen to the surface—*Lectio Divina,* or "divine reading." *Lectio* is a simple, four-step process of listening for God's voice as you move through a short passage of Scripture.

And this simple, ancient way of reading the library of Scripture has the potential to change your experience of Scripture for a lifetime.

---

* Dietrich Bonhoeffer, *Meditating on the Word* (Lanham, MD: Rowman & Littlefield, 2008), 122.

Reflection Questions

When instructed, circle up in triads (smaller groups of three to five people) and discuss the following questions:

01 How did the church tradition you grew up in or were saved into teach you to engage with Scripture?

02 Share about your experience of finding a place and time to engage with Scripture. How did it go?

03 Did you experience delight, restlessness, frustration, or other emotions as you engaged in this Practice?

04 What questions are you holding as you enter into the next part of our Practice?

Teaching

Key Scripture

He said to them, "How foolish you are, and how slow to believe all that the prophets have spoken! Did not the Messiah have to suffer these things and then enter his glory?" And beginning with Moses and all the Prophets, he explained to them what was said in all the Scriptures concerning himself. . . .

"Everything must be fulfilled that is written about me in the Law of Moses, the Prophets and the Psalms." Then he opened their minds so they could understand the Scriptures.

—Luke 24v25–27, 44–45

Session summary

- Today we might call it the Bible or the Old Testament, but Jesus called it "the Law of Moses, the Prophets, and the Psalms"* to communicate the three major divisions of the Hebrew Scriptures:

  - The Law (Genesis–Deuteronomy)

  - The Prophets (starting with Joshua)

  - The Psalms or Writings (wisdom literature and other miscellaneous writings)

- Joshua 1 and Psalm 1 are "canonical seams," literary bridges that connect the Law, Prophets, and Psalms together. They reveal *how* we're invited to read and approach Scripture.

- Both of the passages that make up the canonical seams call us to *meditate*— using the Hebrew word *hagah*, which means "to murmur" or "growl over," like a lion with its prey or a dog with a bone. The idea here is to *chew* on Scripture, drawing nourishment from it the way we digest food.

- Meditation isn't the finish line; it is only the beginning. The Scripture we reflect on is meant to be embodied—to shape who we are and what we do.

- *Lectio Divina* is a meditative practice that has surfaced throughout church history and follows these four simple steps:

  - **Read:** Notice what stands out in the text.

  - **Meditate:** Let those words settle deeply.

  - **Pray:** Respond to God from the heart.

  - **Contemplate:** Rest in God's presence.

---

* Luke 24v44.

Teaching Notes

As you watch Session 02 together, feel free to use these pages to take notes.

Discussion Questions

Now it's time for a conversation about the teaching. Pause the video for a few minutes to discuss in small groups:

01 Where did you feel challenged or invited as you listened?

02 How is a meditative reading similar or different from the way you currently read Scripture?

03 What are your habits for consuming information (such as news, social media, or podcasts)? How could those habits be influencing the way you approach reading Scripture?

04 What might God's invitation be to you as you embark on this journey?

Practice Notes

As you continue to watch Session 02 together, feel free to use this page to take notes.

Closing Prayer

Take a few deep breaths, become aware of God's presence, and pray this prayer slowly, leaving a short silence between each line.

Father,

Let us savor your heavenly words.

Let us delight in the teachings of your love.

Let us be slow and gentle, not missing any detail.

Let us long for it more than food.

Let it nourish and sustain our souls.

Let it draw us always into you.

Amen.

Exercise

Lectio Divina

- **Like last week, begin by becoming aware of God's presence.**

    - If you can, sit in a comfortable but upright position where you can breathe deeply.

    - Relax your body and feel the ground beneath you.

    - Begin to take some deep, slow breaths to quiet your mind.

    - The first goal is to come to stillness—to let all the distractions fall away and to begin to open your heart to the voice of God.

- **Pray for the Spirit of Jesus to come and meet you.**

- **Choose a short passage to meditate on**, ideally a section of Scripture with natural literary flow, one page max. We recommend you start with a psalm or a section from the Gospels, but follow what's in your heart.

- **Follow the four movements to *Lectio*:**

    - **Read** (*lectio*) the passage slowly, paying close attention to what stands out to you and what you sense the Spirit is highlighting to your mind or heart.

    - **Meditate** (*meditatio*). "Chew" on it. Reread the passage a few more times, and reflect on those words or ideas.

    - **Pray** (*oratio*). Turn what you are hearing into a prayer back to God.

    - **Contemplate** (*contemplatio*). Spend a few minutes sitting in God's presence to reflect on and enjoy his love and attention.

- **Let this be a slow, unhurried portion of your day.** Try to give it at least 20 to 30 minutes.

Reach Exercise

Practice one small act of obedience to what you read.

- Start your day by tuning in to God's voice and listening for his guidance from Scripture over your life.

- Then act on the guidance you receive—whether it's a simple act of love or generosity, or reaching out for forgiveness and mending relationships. Go out and "do it." Afterward, take time to share what stood out to you and pray together.

- Remember, whatever God places on your heart, prioritize obedience.

Practice Reflection

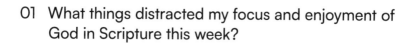

Before your next time together with the group for Session 03, take
10–15 minutes to journal your answers to the following three questions:

01   What things distracted my focus and enjoyment of
     God in Scripture this week?

02   Where did I feel a sense of peace, joy, or anticipation
     as I engaged with Scripture?

03   How did I experience God's love this week?

*Note: As you write, be as specific as possible. While bullet points are fine, if you
write your insights out in narrative form, your brain will be able to process them in a
more lasting way.*

Reflection Notes

Keep Growing (Optional)

The following resources were curated to enhance your experience of this Practice, but they are entirely optional.

📖 Read

Eat This Book by Eugene Peterson (Chapters 03–04)

▶️ Watch

This week, we're continuing BibleProject's How to Read the Bible series with part 02, "How to Read Biblical Narrative" (link.practicingtheway.org /scripture-2). Watch these six episodes to explore the beauty of this literary style and its unique role in the story of Scripture:

- Plot
- Character
- Setting
- Design Patterns
- The Gospel
- The Parables of Jesus

*Please note: These episodes are only a few minutes long, fun to watch, and very helpful in learning to read Scripture.

🎵 Listen

Rule of Life podcast on Scripture (Episode 02)
Join John Mark as he interviews the BibleProject scholar team.

💬 Bonus Conversation

If you would like to slow down this four-week Practice to give your community more time to sit in each week's teaching and spiritual exercise, you can pause and meet for an optional conversation outlined in the appendix.

Study

Overview

The Bible is not a book; it's a library. And it was written thousands of years ago, in three different languages, by dozens of different authors, and in multiple genres of literature. As you would expect, it can be hard to understand at times, and we can easily get lost or turned around as we work through it.

But by reading the teachings of Jesus, it becomes clear that if we *misunderstand* Scripture, it can do great damage to our souls and society. Jesus himself spent a lot of time correcting common misreadings of Scripture. But the reverse is also true: If we *understand* what the library of Scripture is saying to us, it can enlarge and enrich our lives in profound ways.

But for that to happen, we need *study*.

Study is the patient application of our minds and hearts to the process of learning what the text says, what it meant to the original audience, and what it all means for us today.

Often, study doesn't *feel* as "spiritual" as *Lectio Divina* or other ways of engaging Scripture. It can feel academic and dry. But study is a spiritual discipline when it's done for the proper motivation—to know and love God and be formed to be like him.

In this session, we explore the discipline of study.

Reflection Questions

When instructed, circle up in triads (smaller groups of three to five people) and discuss the following questions:

01 What was your experience of engaging with Scripture through *Lectio Divina*?

02 Of the four movements of engaging with Scripture through *Lectio*, which movements felt most natural or challenging to you?

03 What arose in your heart and imagination as you read, meditated, prayed, and contemplated?

04 In the teaching, a fifth movement of "incarnation" was shared. Did you have any opportunities to live out what you were reading this week? If so, how did that deepen the meaning of that Scripture for you?

Teaching

Key Scripture

Jesus, full of the Holy Spirit, left the Jordan and was led by the Spirit into the wilderness, where for forty days he was tempted by the devil. He ate nothing during those days, and at the end of them he was hungry.

The devil said to him, "If you are the Son of God, tell this stone to become bread."

Jesus answered, "It is written: 'Man shall not live on bread alone.'"

The devil led him up to a high place and showed him in an instant all the kingdoms of the world. And he said to him, "I will give you all their authority and splendor; it has been given to me, and I can give it to anyone I want to. If you worship me, it will all be yours."

Jesus answered, "It is written: 'Worship the Lord your God and serve him only.'"

The devil led him to Jerusalem and had him stand on the highest point of the temple. "If you are the Son of God," he said, "throw yourself down from here. For it is written:

"'He will command his angels concerning you
    to guard you carefully;
they will lift you up in their hands,
    so that you will not strike your foot against a stone.'"

Jesus answered, "It is said: 'Do not put the Lord your God to the test.'"

When the devil had finished all this tempting, he left him until an opportune time.

—Luke 4v1–13

Session summary

- Look at how steeped in Scripture Jesus was. His words and actions were saturated in Scripture—so much so that his automatic response to the accuser's lies was to quote Scripture.

- Look at how cunning the devil was with Scripture. This shows us how easily the Bible can be twisted and misinterpreted. When it's not properly understood, Scripture can be—and sadly has been—weaponized against others, causing great harm to society.

- How do we avoid this? The key is to intentionally incorporate the discipline of study into our ongoing lives with God.

- Study is the patient application of our minds and hearts to the process of learning what the text says, what it meant to the original audience, and what it all means for us today.

- The reality is that Scripture is hard to read because of four challenges:
  - Written in other languages
  - Written in other times and cultures
  - Authored by many writers in various genres
  - Written over 1,500 years but part of a unified story that leads to Jesus

- Here are four study tips we recommend:
  - Place yourself under gifted, trusted teachers.
  - Build a library.
  - Pick an area of study in your season.
  - Don't go it alone.

- Our motivation for studying Scripture must always be love. The deeper we dive into its truths, the more we come to know, understand, and love the one it's all about—Jesus.

Teaching Notes

As you watch Session 03 together, feel free to use these pages to take notes.

Discussion Questions

Now it's time for a conversation about the teaching. Pause the video for a few minutes to discuss in small groups:

01 As you listened, what resonated with your heart and mind? Were there moments you experienced resistance or your perspective was challenged?

02 What is one word to describe your initial feeling toward the idea of studying Scripture (e.g., duty, curiosity, overwhelm, etc.)? Why did you choose that word?

03 Who is an example of someone in your life who has been positively formed through the study of Scripture? What do you want to consider from their example as you approach studying Scripture this week?

04 If studying Scripture risks becoming about intellectual curiosity rather than fostering a deeper love for Jesus, what signs can help us recognize when we are leaning toward one or the other?

Practice Notes

As you continue to watch Session 03 together, feel free to use this page to take notes.

Closing Prayer

End your time together by praying this liturgy:

Your wisdom, Lord, is deep and vast.
It's beyond our comprehension,
yet you have said, "If anyone has ears to hear,
let them hear."* Give us ears and minds that can
listen and understand.
Guide us, keep us from error and discouragement,
and show us the path to everlasting life.
To see and know you, we need you.

Amen.

---

* Mark 4v23.

Exercise

Study

- **First, choose a passage or theme of Scripture.** Ideally, select one that you find your heart drawn to but don't yet understand or one that you feel an aversion to, either because you don't understand it or because you're scared you do.

- **Study it in a thoughtful, loving, and prayerful way.** Here are a few ways you can study your chosen passage:
  - Listen to teaching(s) on the passage.
  - Watch an overview of the passage on BibleProject.com.
  - Utilize a study Bible. Follow the notes and footnotes connected to that passage.
  - Read through a few commentaries or study resources. We have a helpful list of suggestions in the appendix for you.
  - Attend a Bible study or class through your church or online through BibleProject Classroom (link.practicingtheway.org/scripture-3a).

- **Start your own library.** You may want to begin with the following resources:
  - A study Bible
  - A Bible dictionary
  - A commentary set
  - A book or two on hermeneutics

  For specific suggestions, see our recommended reading lists in the Continue the Journey section of this Guide on pages 102–105.

- As you study, here are a few tips:

  01 Study with your whole heart, not just your left brain. Pray before, during, and after. Pause when you are moved by an idea or insight, and let it seep into you deeply and spill into conversation with God.

  02 Take notes. Write down what you learn.

  03 Share your insights with someone else, as the act of speaking out what you learn leaves an imprint on your memory.

Reach Exercise

Begin reading a piece of literary fiction.

It might sound strange at first, but remember that Scripture is meditation literature. So with this Reach Exercise, the idea is that by learning how to read literary art, you'll be better equipped to read Scripture too.

Below are a few of our top recommendations:

- *Island of the World* by Michael O'Brien

- *Gilead* by Marilynne Robinson

- *East of Eden* by John Steinbeck

- *Their Eyes Were Watching God* by Zora Neale Hurston

- *The Lord of the Rings* trilogy by J.R.R. Tolkien

- *The Violent Bear It Away* by Flannery O'Connor

- *The Brothers Karamazov* by Fyodor Dostoyevsky

Short stories:

- *The Death of Ivan Ilyich* by Leo Tolstoy

- *Chronicle of a Death Foretold* by Gabriel García Márquez

- *Leaf by Niggle* by J.R.R. Tolkien

Note that, like the Bible itself, some of these works of literature have episodes of sexuality and violence. Even as we direct our minds to meditate upon "whatever is true, whatever is noble, whatever is right,"* we find value in exploring the human condition through literature.

---

* Philippians 4v8.

Practice Reflection

Before your next time together with the group for Session 04, take 10–15 minutes to journal your answers to the following three questions:

01 How do I feel God challenging me to grow through this Practice?

02 How can I cultivate more joy in my times of study?

03 In what ways did I experience God's presence as I studied?

Note: As you write, be as specific as possible. While bullet points are fine, if you write your insights out in narrative form, your brain will be able to process them in a more lasting way.

Reflection Notes

Keep Growing (Optional)

The following resources were curated to enhance your experience of this Practice, but they are entirely optional.

📖 Read

Eat This Book by Eugene Peterson (Chapters 05–06)

▶ Watch

This week, we're continuing BibleProject's How to Read the Bible series with part 03, "How to Read Biblical Poetry" (link.practicingtheway.org /scripture-3b). Watch these six short episodes to learn how this style is used to communicate approximately 30 percent of Scripture.

- Poetry
- Poetic Metaphor
- The Book of Psalms
- The Prophets
- The Books of Solomon
- Apocalyptic Literature

*Please note: These episodes are only a few minutes long, fun to watch, and very helpful in learning to read Scripture.

ᵢ|ᵢ|ᵢ Listen

Rule of Life podcast on Scripture (Episode 03)
Join John Mark as he interviews the BibleProject scholar team.

💬 Bonus Conversation

If you would like to slow down this four-week Practice to give your community more time to sit in each week's teaching and spiritual exercise, you can pause and meet for an optional conversation outlined in the appendix.

Memorize

Overview

Jesus' final words on the cross were a quote from Psalm 22v1: "My God, my God, why have you forsaken me?" When he was under pressure, when his soul was crushed, what came out of him wasn't fear or rage or blame—it was Scripture. The rich, poetic imagination of a thousand-year-old Messianic prophecy became the lens through which he interpreted his pain and suffering.

The memorization of Scripture can do the same for us—it can anchor us in God's presence, purposes, and peace through all our days, including the seasons when our souls (or even our bodies) are in the throes of pain and suffering.

In the digital age, most of us have long abandoned the practice of memorization. Few of us could even recite our best friends' phone numbers. Why store that information in our brains when we can store it in the cloud? Why put in the work to memorize a Scripture when we can just google it? But this ancient practice of storing the truths of God so deep in our bodies they are there when we most need them simply cannot be done by a device.

And as we build an inner library of key texts that we have put to memory (over many years of following Jesus), these texts begin to rewire our brains, causing us to take on the "mind of Christ."*

---

* 1 Corinthians 2v16.

Reflection Questions

When instructed, circle up in triads (smaller groups of three to five people) and discuss the following questions:

01 Which passage or theme in Scripture did you choose to study and why?

02 How did this passage or theme grow in meaning from when you started your study to when you completed it?

03 Was it challenging to engage your heart as you studied? What emotions, if any, surfaced as you did?

04 In what ways does this passage or theme relate to you personally? How has it impacted the way you think about your life right now?

Teaching

Key Scripture

From noon until three in the afternoon darkness came over all the land. About three in the afternoon Jesus cried out in a loud voice, *"Eli, Eli, lema sabachthani?"* (which means "My God, my God, why have you forsaken me?").

—Matthew 27v45–46

Session summary

- Jesus' cry in Matthew 27 is often misunderstood as doubt, but it is actually quoting an ancient prophecy from Psalm 22.

- Jesus masterfully employed *remez*, an ancient Hebrew technique steeped in oral tradition. By quoting just one line in a familiar passage, he meant to spark a chain reaction in his listeners' minds, inviting them to recall the entire text and its full meaning.

- Psalm 22 explains King David's experiences but also foreshadows Jesus' suffering and divine mission. By quoting this Scripture, Jesus was telling us exactly who he was—the ultimate Messianic King promised to come in the Davidic line.

- If Jesus needed to put Scripture to memory, *how much more so do you and I?*

- Here are four things Scripture memorization can help us do:
  - Hear God's voice.
  - Renew our minds.
  - Resist temptation.
  - Draw on God's strength in seasons of pain and suffering.

- The goal is for God's thoughts to become deeply imprinted on our minds so that in both challenging times and moments of joy, we begin to think and feel as he does, seeing the world through his eyes and responding as he would if he were us.

Teaching Notes

As you watch Session 04 together, feel free to use these pages to take notes.

Discussion Questions

Now it's time for a conversation about the teaching. Pause the video for a few minutes to discuss in small groups:

01 As you listened, what most stood out to you?

02 How have you experienced the truth of "you are what you contemplate" or "you become what you meditate on"?

03 If you could share only one insight or reflection that you want to internalize going forward from this Practice, what would it be?

04 Reflecting on the past few weeks in this Practice, how has your relationship with Scripture changed?

Practice Notes

As you continue to watch Session 04 together, feel free to use this page to take notes.

Closing Prayer

End your time together by praying this liturgy:

Living God, whose word is living,
active, articulate, and true,
may your words live always in us,
taking hold of and illuminating us,
so that as we carry them in the
wombs of our souls, they may
enlighten the world with you.
Amen.

Exercise

Memorizing a passage of Scripture

- **Identify a short passage you want to put to memory.**
  - Here are some recommendations for you:
    - Galatians 5v22–23
    - Ephesians 4v29–30
    - Philippians 4v6–7
    - Colossians 3v23–24
    - James 3v16–17
    - 2 Peter 1v3–4
    - 1 John 4v15–16
  - No pressure to choose from this list. It is best if you choose a Scripture that your heart is drawn toward.
  - Make sure the passage is short enough to memorize in one week.

- **Every single day for a week, work on memorization, and after seven days you should be able to recite the passage from memory.**

- **Here are five best practices:**
  - **Read it out loud.** Every day. Four times in a row.
  - **Write it out by hand** to activate your motor neurons and embed it in your brain more deeply. Then, every day memorize from your paper.
  - **Visualize it.** Close your eyes and connect an image to the sentence you are working on. Imagine yourself in the story.
  - **Recite it.** This is called "active recall." Every day push your brain to recite a little more of it from memory and not from reading.
  - **Recite it to another person.**

- **Here are more tips from the leading science on memorization:**
  - **Be consistent:** Memorization takes regular practice. Set a time each day to work on it.

- ○ **Study:** The more you understand a passage, the easier it is to remember.
- ○ **Paraphrase:** Put the verses into your own words to deepen comprehension.
- ○ **Teach:** Explain the passage to someone—or even just to yourself—out loud or in writing.
- ○ **Sleep:** Real memory work happens while you sleep. Try reviewing before bed to lock it in.

- **Keep the Scripture in your memory.**
  - ○ Review once a day for at least a month.
  - ○ Then review once a week for a year.
  - ○ Then review once a month for the rest of your life.
  - ○ This will require a system. Choose a simple one that will work for you—maybe index cards and a little box organizer, a calendar appointment and reminder, or an organization app on your phone.

Reach Exercise

Memorize an entire passage.

Identify a psalm or a larger passage of Scripture that has been especially meaningful to you in this season of your life.

- Over the coming weeks, put the entire passage to memory.
- We recommend you take on about two verses a week. Follow the same process as above for as many weeks as it takes to memorize the passage.

Practice Reflection

Take 10–15 minutes to journal your answers to the following three questions:

01 What prayer or deep desire came up in my heart as I memorized this week?

02 Where did calling Scripture to mind bring me peace or direction?

03 How did I experience God this week through memorization?

Note: As you write, be as specific as possible. While bullet points are fine, if you write your insights out in narrative form, your brain will be able to process them in a more lasting way.

Reflection Notes

Keep Growing (Optional)

The following resources were curated to enhance your experience of this Practice, but they are entirely optional.

📖 Read

Eat This Book by Eugene Peterson (Chapters 07–09)

▶️ Watch

This week, we complete BibleProject's How to Read the Bible series with part 04, "How to Read Biblical Prose Discourse" (link.practicingtheway.org /scripture-4). Watch these three short episodes to learn more about this genre.

- Biblical Law
- New Testament Letters: Historical Context
- New Testament Letters: Literary Context

*Please note: These episodes are only a few minutes long, fun to watch, and very helpful in learning to read Scripture.

ᴵᴵᴵᴵᴵ Listen

Rule of Life podcast on Scripture (Episode 04)
Join John Mark as he interviews the BibleProject scholar team.

💬 Bonus Conversation (Optional)

If you would like to slow down this four-week Practice to give your community more time to sit in each week's teaching and spiritual exercise, you can pause and meet for an optional conversation outlined in the appendix.

May God open your mind to understand the Scriptures.

May your hearts burn as you read.

And may you meet Jesus on every page.

PART 03

Continue the Journey

Recommended Reading

Reading Scripture isn't just a daily discipline; it's a lifetime journey. We can spend decades in this library and just scratch the surface.

Here are some of our favorite books on reading Scripture as a spiritual discipline, for those of you who desire to learn more:

***Experiencing Scripture as a Disciple of Jesus: Reading the Bible like Dallas Willard* by Dave Ripper**
Introduces readers to Dallas Willard's unique approach to spiritual formation—transforming Bible reading from mere study into a profound, experiential encounter with God.

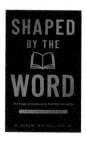

***Shaped by the Word: The Power of Scripture in Spiritual Formation* by M. Robert Mulholland, Jr.**
Guides readers to transform Bible study into a life-changing encounter with God by teaching them to listen for his voice and engage with Scripture in a way that fosters true spiritual formation.

Opening to God: Lectio Divina and Life as Prayer
by David G. Benner

Teaches the four movements of *Lectio Divina*, inviting readers
to move beyond viewing prayer as an obligation and into a
transformative communion with God.

The Blue Parakeet: Rethinking How You Read the Bible
by Scot McKnight

Challenges conservatives and liberals to stop taming the Bible
and embrace a fresh reading that transcends old debates and
speaks to today's generation.

Here are some of our favorite books on hermeneutics—the art and science of biblical interpretation:

Read the Bible for a Change: Understanding and Responding to God's Word **by Ray Lubeck**

Equips readers with practical tools to deeply engage with Scripture, addressing the relevance of biblical passages for today while guiding readers in understanding context, literary styles, and life-changing truths.

How to Read the Bible for All Its Worth **by Gordon D. Fee and Douglas Stuart**

Offers essential insights for interpreting Scripture, helping readers navigate its diverse literary styles to uncover its intended meaning.

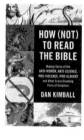

How (Not) to Read the Bible: Making Sense of the Anti-Women, Anti-Science, Pro-Violence, Pro-Slavery and Other Crazy-Sounding Parts of Scripture **by Dan Kimball**

Addresses tough questions and misconceptions about the Bible, providing a guide for both Christians and skeptics to navigate its puzzling and often disturbing passages while reaffirming its value as a moral and spiritual text.

Misreading Scripture with Western Eyes: Removing Cultural Blinders to Better Understand the Bible **by E. Randolph Richards and Brandon J. O'Brien**

Reveals how cultural biases can distort our understanding of Scripture, urging us to consider the original context to gain a clearer view of the Bible's messages.

Here are some of our favorite resources for biblical study:

Bestcommentaries.com
A well-curated list of the best commentaries on each book of the Bible.

BibleProject Book Overviews
Visual summaries that break down the key themes and structures of each book of the Bible.

Blueletterbible.org
A free online tool that gives you access to multiple Bible translations, commentaries, word studies, and original languages.

Biblegateway.com
A free platform with multiple translations, keyword searches, and study resources for easy Bible reference.

ESV Study Bible
Provides detailed notes, cross-references, and theological insights with a focus on traditional Christian doctrines.

NIV Cultural Backgrounds Study Bible
Offers historical, cultural, and geographical context to help you see Scripture through the eyes of its original audience.

The IVP Bible Background Commentary
Explains the cultural and historical background of ancient customs, practices, and daily life in both the Old and New Testaments.

The New Testament for Everyone series by N. T. Wright
Offers easy-to-read commentary that explains the New Testament in light of both scholarship and faith.

The NIV Application Commentary series
Focuses on how biblical principles can be applied to modern life.

Mounce's Complete Expository Dictionary of Old and New Testament Words
Provides in-depth word studies, definitions, and explanations to increase understanding of key biblical terms in their original languages.

About BibleProject

Throughout this Practice we utilized the world-class resources of BibleProject, and we highly recommend you continue to draw on their work as you move forward on your spiritual journey.

BibleProject is a nonprofit, crowdfunded organization that makes free resources like videos, podcasts, articles, and classes to help people experience the Bible in a way that is approachable and transformative.

The Practices

Information alone isn't enough to produce transformation.

By adopting not just the teaching but also the practices from Jesus' own life, we open up our entire beings to God and allow him to transform us into people of love.

Our nine core Practices work together to form a Rule of Life for the modern era.

Sabbath	**Prayer**	**Fasting**
Solitude	**Generosity**	**Scripture**
Community	**Service**	**Witness**

WHAT'S INCLUDED FOR EACH PRACTICE

Four Sessions

Each session includes teaching, guided discussion, and weekly exercises to integrate the Practices into daily life.

Companion Guide

A detailed guide provides question prompts, session-by-session exercises, and space to write and reflect.

Recommended Resources

Additional recommended readings and podcasts offer a way to get the most out of the Practices.

Learn more by visiting practicingtheway.org/resources.

The Scripture Practice

The Practicing the Way Course

An eight-session primer on spiritual formation.

Two thousand years ago, Jesus said to his disciples, "Follow me." But what does it mean for us to follow Jesus today?

The Practicing the Way Course is an on-ramp to spiritual formation, exploring what it means to follow Jesus and laying the foundation for a life of apprenticeship to him.

WHAT'S INCLUDED

Eight Sessions

John Mark and other voices teaching on apprenticing under Jesus, spiritual formation, healing from sin, meeting God in pain, crafting a Rule of Life, living in community, and more

Exercises

Weekly practices and exercises to help integrate what you've learned into your everyday life

Guided Conversation

Prompts to reflect on your experience and process honestly in community

Companion Guide

A detailed workbook with exercises, space to write and reflect, and suggestions for supplemental resources

Learn more by visiting practicingtheway.org/resources.

Practicing the Way:
Be with him. Become like him. Do as he did.

The first followers of Jesus developed a Rule of Life, or habits and practices based on the life of Jesus himself. As they learned to live like their teacher, they became people who made space for God to do his most transformative work in their lives.

Practicing the Way is a vision for the future, shaped by the wisdom of the past. It's an introduction to spiritual formation accessible to both beginners and lifelong followers of Jesus and a companion to the Practicing the Way Course (practicingtheway.org/course). This book offers theological substance, astute cultural insight, and practical wisdom for creating a Rule of Life (practicingtheway .org/ruleoflifebuilder) in the modern age.

You can order your copy or get copies for your community at practicingtheway.org/book or through your preferred bookseller.

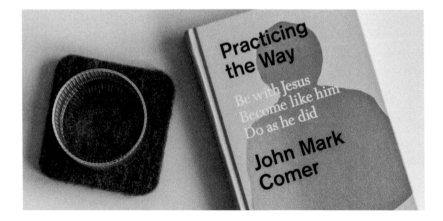

The Scripture Practice

The Circle

Practicing the Way is a nonprofit that develops spiritual formation resources for churches and small groups learning how to become apprentices in the Way of Jesus.

We believe one of the greatest needs of our time is for people to discover how to become lifelong disciples of Jesus. To that end, we help people learn how to be with Jesus, become like him, and do as he did, through the practices and rhythms he and his earliest followers lived by.

All of our downloadable ministry resources are available at no cost, thanks to the generosity of The Circle and other givers from around the world who partner with us to see formation integrated into the Church at large.

To learn more or join us, visit practicingtheway.org/give.

For Facilitators

Before you begin, there are three easy things you need to do (this should take only 10–15 minutes).

01   Go to launch.practicingtheway.org, log in, create a group, and send a digital invitation to your community. This will give your group access to the Spiritual Health Reflection, videos, and all sorts of valuable extras. Encourage your group to bring along their Companion Guides to each session, as these contain the discussion questions and space to take notes.

- You can purchase a print or ebook version from your preferred book retailer. We recommend the print version so you can stay away from your devices during the Practices, as well as take notes during each session. But we realize that digital works better for some.

- Note: You can order the Guides ahead of time and have them waiting when people arrive for Session 01, or encourage people to order or download their own and bring them to your gatherings.

02   Send a message to your group encouraging everyone to take the Spiritual Health Reflection before your first gathering. You can direct your group to practicingtheway.org/reflection.

03   If your group has not been through the Practicing the Way Course, invite them to watch the short primer in the online Dashboard before you gather for Session 01 of this Practice.

For training, tips, and more resources for facilitating the Scripture Practice, log in to the Dashboard at launch.practicingtheway.org.

APPENDIX

Bonus Conversations

Read

Paul's words to Timothy are about persevering in faith within a world often at odds with the Way of Jesus. Here, he invites Timothy (and us) into a resilience rooted deeply in purpose, truth, and the transformative power of Scripture. For Paul, Scripture wasn't just ink on a page; it was the very breath of God, capable of reshaping him into the person he was created to be.

You, however, know all about my teaching, my way of life, my purpose, faith, patience, love, endurance, persecutions, sufferings—what kinds of things happened to me in Antioch, Iconium and Lystra, the persecutions I endured. Yet the Lord rescued me from all of them. In fact, everyone who wants to live a godly life in Christ Jesus will be persecuted, while evildoers and impostors will go from bad to worse, deceiving and being deceived. But as for you, continue in what you have learned and have become convinced of, because you know those from whom you learned it, and how from infancy you have known the Holy Scriptures, which are able to make you wise for salvation through faith in Christ Jesus.

All Scripture is God-breathed and is useful for teaching, rebuking, correcting and training in righteousness, so that the servant of God may be thoroughly equipped for every good work.

—2 Timothy 3v10–17

Discuss the Scripture

01   What do you notice as you read the Scripture passage?

02   We often read 2 Timothy 3v16 by itself. How does your understanding of this verse expand when you consider its context?

03   Paul gives Timothy a heads-up that anyone serious about following Jesus will encounter opposition (v12). Have you experienced this in your own journey?

04   List the ways Paul describes Scripture as useful for equipping us for "every good work." What other things do you rely on for guidance and strength? What might it look like to truly prioritize Scripture in this way?

Discuss the practice

01   Think back to a season of struggle in your life. What Scriptures helped shape and steady you through that time?

02   Paul encourages Timothy to keep living in what he's come to believe deeply. Discuss one specific truth from Scripture that you're convinced of. Why are you convinced?

03   What would it look like for you to approach Scripture as God-breathed rather than just a text to be studied?

04   Paul describes Scripture as equipping us "for every good work." Where might God be inviting you to join him in a "good work" in your community, family, or friendships?

Meditate

Read this introduction and Scripture together before discussing.

Psalm 1 serves as a pivotal bridge between the Prophets and the Writings, offering profound insight into how we should approach all of Scripture through the lens of meditation.

The psalm paints a picture of the blessed person, who not only steers clear of godless and selfish behaviors but also delights in the law of the Lord, meditating on it day and night. As we contemplate this passage, let's reflect on the voices and influences that are shaping our lives. Are we genuinely rooting ourselves in Scripture, allowing it to nourish our souls?

Blessed is the one
    who does not walk in step with the wicked
or stand in the way that sinners take
    or sit in the company of mockers,
but whose delight is in the law of the Lord,
    and who meditates on his law day and night.
That person is like a tree planted by streams of water,
    which yields its fruit in season
and whose leaf does not wither—
    whatever they do prospers.

—Psalm 1:1–3

Discuss the Scripture

01   Take note of what a blessed person does every day. How does that expand your understanding of what it means to live "blessed"?

02   What does the blessed person avoid? Take note: *Wicked, sinners,* and *mockers* aren't just labels; they reflect attitudes and choices that can pull us away from God. In your experience, what does it practically look like to steer clear of these influences?

03   Reflect on the Hebrew word for meditate, *hagah* ("to murmur," or "to growl over" like a lion over its food). How can meditation on Scripture be like savoring your favorite meal?

04   Think about the creative analogy presented in verse 3. How is a person delighting in Scripture daily like a tree planted by water?

Discuss the practice

01   How do you approach meditation right now?

02   What challenges do you face in staying consistent with your meditation?

03   The psalmist invites us to delight in the law of the Lord. How can we infuse more joy into our times with Scripture each day?

04   Meditation shapes identity—our imaginations, beliefs, thoughts, and actions. Can you think of a specific truth from Scripture that has transformed your life? Share that with your group.

Study

Read this introduction and Scripture together before discussing.

In his letter to the Romans, Paul envisions a community that is deeply rooted in the Scriptures. For Paul, these texts are not just relics of the past; they are the foundation for our lives today. When he says, "Everything that was written in the past was written to teach us," he's highlighting how the Scriptures serve as a road map for endurance and hope.

We who are strong ought to bear with the failings of the weak and not to please ourselves. Each of us should please our neighbors for their good, to build them up. For even Christ did not please himself but, as it is written: "The insults of those who insult you have fallen on me." For everything that was written in the past was written to teach us, so that through the endurance taught in the Scriptures and the encouragement they provide we might have hope.

May the God who gives endurance and encouragement give you the same attitude of mind toward each other that Christ Jesus had, so that with one mind and one voice you may glorify the God and Father of our Lord Jesus Christ.

—Romans 15v1–6

Discuss the Scripture

01   What stands out to you as you read the Scripture passage?

02   Paul quotes Psalm 69v9 to highlight an example of endurance and offer encouragement. Take a moment to read the entire psalm. What stands out to you about endurance in Psalm 69? How does reading Psalm 69 in context color your interpretation of Romans 15?

03   Think about a current challenge you're facing. How can reflecting on examples of faithful suffering in Psalm 69 (or other portions of Scripture) provide hope and help you endure to love others?

04   Look closely at what comes after "so that" in Romans 15v6. Why does Paul say that God gives us endurance and encouragement through Scripture? Discuss how this is significant.

Discuss the practice

01   How does studying Scripture in community impact your encouragement and hope?

02   Can you share a personal experience where studying a specific passage of Scripture provided you with endurance, encouragement, or hope during a challenging time?

03   What are some things we can develop in our group that would help us deepen our collective engagement with Scripture and invite even richer conversations?

04   What are some other practical ways we can embody "one mind and one voice" in our conversations and interactions to live out the unity that Paul invites us into in this passage?

Memorize

In Psalm 19, we catch a profound glimpse of how God's commands and principles provide guidance and health to our souls. The psalmist revels in the wisdom of God's statutes, painting them as trustworthy, radiant, and life-giving. God's instructions aren't just rules to follow; they are a wellspring of spiritual renewal.

The law of the LORD is perfect,
  refreshing the soul.
The statutes of the LORD are trustworthy,
  making wise the simple.
The precepts of the LORD are right,
  giving joy to the heart.
The commands of the LORD are radiant,
  giving light to the eyes.
The fear of the LORD is pure,
  enduring forever.
The decrees of the LORD are firm,
  and all of them are righteous.

They are more precious than gold,
  than much pure gold;
they are sweeter than honey,
  than honey from the honeycomb.

By them your servant is warned;
  in keeping them there is great reward.
But who can discern their own errors?
  Forgive my hidden faults.
Keep your servant also from willful sins;
  may they not rule over me.
Then I will be blameless,
  innocent of great transgression.

May these words of my mouth and this meditation of my heart
  be pleasing in your sight,
  LORD, my Rock and my Redeemer.

—Psalm 19v7–14

Discuss the Scripture

01   Observe the ways the psalmist describes the commands, statutes (laws), precepts (principles), and decrees (orders or decisions) of the Lord. What stands out to you?

02   The psalmist treasures God's orders and decisions as more precious than gold and sweeter than honey. What value do you place on them in your own life, and how do they affect your daily choices?

03   Reflect on verses 12 and 13. Discuss the relationship between receiving God's forgiveness and being named blameless and innocent. What does this tell us about God's character?

04   Pay attention to the last verse (v14). What is the psalmist's prayer and desire? Note how the psalmist addresses the Lord: "my Rock and my Redeemer." Discuss the significance of these things together.

Discuss the practice

01   What is one small step you can take to weave Scripture memorization into your current daily habits?

02   What intrigues you most about the idea of memorizing Scripture, and what are your hopes for how it will begin (or continue) to shape your life?

03   Let's talk about how memorizing Scripture helps us navigate temptation in our lives. Share a time when a specific verse guided you through a tough situation. Or share a Scripture that is helping you through a current tough situation.

04   Let's talk about how memorizing Scripture can shape our understanding of God's character and his promises. Share a specific verse that has changed the way you see God. Or share a Scripture that you need right now in order to understand God in a new light.

To inquire about ordering this Companion Guide in
bulk quantities for your church, small group, or staff,
contact churches@penguinrandomhouse.com.